The Unordering of Days

The Unordering of Days

Poems

Jessica Palmer

atmosphere press

Table of Contents

After the Parameters

The theory contends
Offer myself to
The world will
Wrap its hydrogen
Around me like a song
Or maybe even a
Nitrogen web but not

like a fig Enveloping
a wasp Consuming
sharper blurred Edges
for its own Cloying
purpose decomposes Into
an auxiliary carbon so My
oxygen defines Another
not me. I used to Enjoy
figs. I wanted to be Loved,
but not like this. Not

like an inverted flower
pretending to be our
Most Succulent Fruit

Retraction

it is a closing is it not an
endearment to wish this way or that
upon the flattened zephyr. to factory
yourself an electron in split ask the
everlasting question what
are you doing here is
the sum of all things
a thousand pieces minus

when voiding forgiveness there
is nowhere the sound can travel in
you and through you centimeter
away to unearth the salient points. did
I bury myself deep enough thickets
spliced by border walls. we are
composed of spaces between
spaces, until it is time to

turn ourselves into finally ourselves

I had a mouth once. it
opened wide like a chickadee, like
regret

the Ecstatic

when did I build a late   room to insulate torrents
against the screen   tilting into expanse the
ecstatic and you will be   for me a hurricane and I will
be for you new eyes I lean into   your openness and fall against
earthed prose touching   the darkness we once touched
my weight of emptiness my   jaw-worn temptations solving
courtesies imbibing distance   into algorithms of wrung hope is it not
enough to altar my certainty   must you also make me live in it

For One the Repetitions

And what held the balance of lives, ivy swindling
through branches, stains removed from
walls in record time, dust veils swept under
bookshelves. Trees unnamed. Ants are

heavy this year. What again was I doing
with my days? Arrange bundles, stack cans,
drag my nails across a quarter's circumference,
this furious caution binding joy to vision, twice

unmarrowed from contained loneliness. It is,
perhaps, for the best that the failure of language
ruptures inward, a rivet of clay melting eddies
of foam and grain. There are essentials, but

I never reach them, insisting on civil thanks that
are not generosity but desperation split in three
halves. Portioning restraint into poised slivers of need.
Off the hillside, hushed into the brevity of mountains.

And the Things We Have Left Undone

At eight I summoned the Holy Ghost in a next
door room with the glottals of abandon, the gutturals
of syncopated language. I invited Him in to

pour forth a confluence of desire and nonsense I
haven't spoken sense. At eighteen doubt caused every
failing of every prophet every king but

when a chit of a girl heralded questions were no
sin, the message cocooned himself in borrowed masculinity.
Last year I rifted the mountains and hallowed

how much I hated and unprayed the horseshoe marks in
the clay trail were deep enough to cover my flagellation. They
say the Holy Spirit lives in me, but I think He lives

under me as I barter down to sheerings of acquiescence.
Yesterday we sanctified our prayerlessness, speaking
guilt and time and unworthy, yet I mootly

redact boredom and confusion and what if we're praying to nothing,
but these are not audible options. And Oh He Is a Gentleman, so I
push Him under twice beneath me, His

force the weight of all the drugs I never took, the men I never
slept with, the absence of hungover mornings. The virtue I market
with my lack of action. To look upon the creation

of Myself and declare it good. While others have had a falling out
in the Spirit, the Two of Us have just fallen out, our different forces
spanning such unreachable. I tried to learn his

language but wonder if he'd risk hearing mine.

In Advance of Reproval

it is not that my thoughts
are unthinkable, it is that
I have mistaken your hands
for a fish. for a fragiled
hesitation. what small
apologies I make to level
abyssals, what ways I would
grow to your height, breach
your eyes and demand a
return of my slendered mitosis.
I would stand on
    this cushion
    this stool
    this wave
as you pretend one person
to love, but that is not even
yourself. I have unwanted
you so long it has become
a sabbath. a fish at my arms,
in my arms. one can only
hold so much in a hand before
all beliefs are meant to be broken.

Myopia

I have not arrived at half myself,
Have not carved refracted air
Into one continuous motion of
Clayed earth, opened palms

I have consolationed a million
Ways to despair a creature
Pluck her feathers from their follicles
Forget she waits to breathe

Again. Do we know where darkness
Leads? To light upon light, but
I prefer to asunder my past, colliding
Transparencies instead of present you

I have discerned to modernize my needs,
Compress them into tight pillars of salt. To
Untranslate oblivion, as if language alone
Were enough to determine truth. As if
Words were finite, and responsible.

Lunared Anomalies

and we chased larger moons under sky-scrimmed
Appalachia, misplacing cracked understanding
for lingering ranges, their jagged, gentled
angles the backscape for my pause in Clarity. the world
swollen with erosion and summoning, and I followed a narrow
swath of reckoning unto Myself.

forgive Me. I strove to be

better than This. this lunared anomaly, that manifest twilight
convexed into infinite circles we can't seem to Close. I keep
stomping down the tunnels of moles, pretending I had spoken
Differently. knowing it doesn't make a Difference. I will always
be older than you, than these forged Blue Ridge Ruts. there is no
precise moment of Undoing. only the mired Faltering.

Docilities

approximate earth

shunts a source untraceable, this light bent to matchless grace horizoning
synthesis, *I am a viable means of meridians*, I tell myself, long ago, a
reflection of currency *I am a viable* forfeit of expenditure without
oblation, unspoken pleading this witness *I am* repeats to more
lissome figures approach, *I* a vestige tumefied, speak again
I into the clay grasping for breath of mass to enter, lost
in the alacrity of disguise, acres grown into spires of
tight glory we furrowed into existence, ablaze,
wet sand and purity, I once knew someone
to hold a self apart in permanent stasis
as a state of transition would the
immutable whole relent

opened aside to enclose
everywhere fog on the river dawn
fireflies pressing mountain trees straw
berry moon pulling on Atlantic whispering
no. then to polestar control beneath unseen stars.
waiting for trees unblinking, their rhythm a cataclysm
on new worship. who is the jutting bone of a hip, an organ
at entire disposal. what fallow remnants I have to offer, supine
with mist-rattled embarrassment. listen to the same song on repeat.
remember the sound of a door locking. consumed like sic and no other
reversals burst inward, re-earthing hope and all lights. be closed opened
again the closing is no more a desolate sort of presence no more to subdue

aubaded euphoria

Violences

For to Speak of Unclosing

You forget to ask why
Always, always the rhododendron
That transplants itself along the ridge
In order to achieve formal glory.
You say you have touched the wind and
Then tasted it, but there is no such
Former existence as impossibilities
Imbued with beauty. I did, I did taste
The wind you insist I ask how
It feels and you say salty, which is a lie

Because I shutter to recognize touch.
I have sheathed all the wrong graces
Required against forgiveness. You
Remember it wasn't the
Rhododendron only a brush
Pile of waxy leaves against trout lilies.

The Third [Infinite] Time

Even if you spoke out loud, I wouldn't
Believe you, for I am soft
[Soft] chin, [soft] belly, soft ideas amid
Fissures of dissonant brilliance
    I was [wild]
    once
Ardor unencumbered by small zeitgeists
As you divide hectares of arid crags that
Can't be conquered

You saw me before you saw me, but
I knew your cadence [before speech]
A rush of rebellion to my transience
    perhaps in spent shoes
    perhaps in [vestigial] robes
Whittling away the intricacies of my
Thresholds [brackish beliefs]
Tethering me to nascency as you
Answer the question
[I tried not to ask]
Reciprocity [with]held

Even More of Those Inspirational Catchphrases

My son wants to invent
Portals when he grows up an
Absence of matter takes you
From one place to another or
Traveling beyond the speed of
Light years from now in the vacuum
Dark I will look back at when
I grew up all I wanted was learn

How to sleep how to admit
I don't know the way

But there are no
Portals yet
The distance is so
Far like hot silt the command
Follow your heart is the most pithy
Folly tells my heart to

We Are All of Us Not Scared All the Time I Promise

The hands age first, compelled against
citrused graces of afternoon hunger,
fingers meagered and glassed. Then
the breasts, each dehydrating in accordance
with its need, never so pompous again. Next

the demands the scars to maintain incremental
releases. I was meant for more than this,
I said. Turning, almost hearing,
content to stay in a room, introducing
a continued revival for absolution.

We are all of us not molecules.

What exactly, precisely, particularly is wrong?
Joy, scattered into the words we call abominations.
Humanity crafting idols into its own versions,
interpretations of whims and desires, all my
prepositions on hold, hovering above, beside,
between, during. Against. Into. This is the body
of me, broken for all-I-have-endured-on-my-
own-behalf. Do this in remembrance of me. This
is the cup of the new covenant, poured out for
you-and-the-many-abandonments-of-our-selves.
Do this in remembrance of me. Do this.
At last the eyes but open.

Do this.

We are all of us not stars. Some of the time.

String Theory for Bereavement

Yoke and release energies above
the gradient. Scythe grief through
the stars in reams of inchoate loss,
our gravity of galaxies concising

the collapse. Go, thousand toward
one absolute, one sharing of bliss,
one finding unsolicited obscures me
selfish self-righteous in an escape

or a falling or a failing of sight. Or
what if we remain unrecognized
in the luminous camber of universes.
Unvibrating in the moondust.

I Have Forgotten the Rules of the Multiverse

concave above the inclination of space and
time and matter in omissions of abandon.
reach into galaxies and pull all things to myself
as hesitant alchemy lingers, lifting into arcs of
grandeur. such simple cause and effect without
the nuances of correlation. stand in revolt
against the promise of infinity. this doomsday
reckoning of life in duplicate readily decomposing
into a life in triplicate. those dimensions, those
almost atonements swirling around and through
and into metered, structured chaos, the delusion
being that everything reduces to triangles. when
in reality, opulent, negotiable reality, existence
is more of a jealous, amorphous hendecagon with
a nasty bent toward unmerited retaliation.

I Have Remembered the Rules of the Multiverse

Whatever version given the world,
Whatever version buried within the realm-split
Unhappiness or desires, the excessive
Splendors, the habitual intricacies of
Despair that fill faces with doubt lines
And weeping and againweepingand
Clusterfucksofmisplacednarcissismand

I forgot what I was supposed to be proofing.

Belief does not cull a concept into
Exclusionary existence; that is the eminent
Domain of truth alone. They are not the
Same. This is the language of dispersals
And physics, the only language we have,
And it is

Limited, fashioned to suit our purposes,
Claim understanding, mitigate refusals.
Supplant the ordained.
And the withholding can
Rupture universes.

I Have Rewritten the Rules of the Multiverse

the next moment ephemeraled another hole in the universe as it
shifted left to accommodate the metering of matter into prosaic otherness.
but all strings of the known and

unknown reoriented themselves, particled electricity disquieting
me into awareness, the rendering between those spaces.
the outer atmosphere has

a way of forcing us to abandon pretenses. endless permutations, deaf
causes ripping through the stratosphere, and the question is not
whether this universe will end. the

question is whether it tears, like shredding
fabric, or shatters, like breaking glass
the exquisite of membranes without answer

Rime Ice for November

Ice in November, twice, and to know and
to know these absences wrapped in
plinths of fire. Thus I am constellationed,
points of connection lacking the lines to pull
faith together. In one place a tiger, another
a star-nosed mole searching for pathways
unto themselves. My phone corrects *no stress*
to *monsters* three times a word a phrase
refuses to accompany this sort of presence if
I can't solitude the snow into disruption, yet I
remain. Rime ice crunches off the roof,
sagging to deadened junipers clothed in the
brown needles of all spoken to me without
a word. And we stay longer.

I would very much like to live in a world where
the mistakes I make don't settle like a
hibernation. To unheal a different undoing
each day. Where all these collapses universe
a moment into a single meaning.

***

To have spoken aloud,
To finally say the words, the

Totality of truth. You have
Disappeared into nether. Did

I hallow silence from still
Air? Have I finally disproved

The laws of physics? This
Was my inevitable miracle, to

Create matter where none

Previously existed. So let us say

I am a vulture, let us perceive
My lack of reality for what it is,

Acceptance of a status quo.
Let us now be brave. Let us solely

Speak only the untruths
Others want from us. Is this not a

Life, a good life we have
Manufactured for ourselves? Do you

Not make me laugh? Do I not
Hang up your shirts so they don't shrink

In the dryer, sometimes? Let us
Continue those things, not be lost in

A selection of pretenses. I can Be
Happy, I Promise, I Swear I Promise I'm Happy.

***

As a way of attempting not to cry on Christmas, I have placed a
chocolate in my mouth and called it hope. It is invalid, and all my
transparencies hinge on the precipice.

***

Why yes, indeed, I am in fact a Bad Woman, a
Voice Finder, a Sin Claimer, a Clamor of Dissent.
Did you not know this? Did you forget the stars at
Noon, turn me into nothing more than a fatigable
Explanation? Do not tell me yours is perception
Infallible, that there are no new questions canorous.
What is it that ties us, the tethering of evolution,
Evil to understand the world wrong the wrinkles
On my face and the why. The same why of promises

Slipping from slendered fingers, down drains and
Disposals or under cash registers and aside trails.

I would have presented
You with my horizon if you would have accepted
It, searched for it, the vast expanse of everything we could be.

The louder I swallow, the more I think about how
Loudly I swallow, and this is why I am awake at
Two in the morning. Is there nothing new left to
Dream? For I dream of
My children kidnapped
And hair turning to dust
And the demise of language
And footsteps trapping me in a forged smile
And to wake up next to you
And to terror
And the spinstering of my years.

I would like to dream of
the horizon, an indivisible trust, the impossibility of
Revelations, mitigations placed aside for the first time.

Instead, I will sit on the steps of compacted
belongings, of empathy lost and understanding
refuted, crying out for the life you say I created
ex nihilo. Here is the chair that used to be upstairs.
There is the table that slept next to you, our forms
closing in upon themselves, catalyzed from opposite
Sources. Once more begin.

***

Have you ever
been angry?

Yes.

***

I am
quite sure I have
made you sick
with my absence
of thought. But
now I, too, am
sick, with no one
to bring me tea or
toast. It is nothing
different.

***

I have seen it elsewhere, in a welcoming
back, an acceptance of differences
into a nuanced life. A fervent request for
spring never coming. Children will stand
guard over the world with open generosity,
the strength to proclaim they are enough,
and that is enough. Hold their hands up
to the sky, choosing whether the motion
rejoices or celebrates or says fuck you
to every single person wanting to align them.

So perhaps I am a vulture, feeding on the remains.
Perhaps that is what I was for years, nibbling at
Residual portions of griefdeath. But let us breathe in
New Life, New Space, Unheard of Balance,
Lift our hands to unmake and remake and
remake myself, one to celebrate truth, another
to celebrate truth.

***

It is all of it conjecture, reality

unable to reach your exquisite

absolutes. So we fall, iced

over, glistening in the rime of

respoken wounds, never healing.

Let Us Refuse to Speak of Loneliness

let us refuse to speak of loneliness,
the way it inhales fear like a

wolf, the way it soundtracks a
life into absent ticking of

other notches, disguises as
waiting and waiting a small hope

but mostly more waiting. to have stood
one time in the trees, unencumbered,

bellowed. to have lain upon a floor
too long. these are not the things we say

out loud to ones almost loving us. let us
open our tongues to have them silenced.

No Capacity for Which I Am Unsilenced

a flaxened hollow of
sound, tripping through
the corridors, achieving
balance despite compelled
Otherwisdoms. The

Osmosis made me do it. What
then do we make of peace?

Notes

"Retraction" and "Docilities" first appeared in *Mud Season Review*.

"Myopia," "the Ecstatic," and "Let Us Refuse to Speak of Loneliness" first appeared in *Circle Show*.

"For One the Repetitions" first appeared in *Storyscape*.

"In Advance of Reproval" first appeared in *Epigraph*.

"For to Speak of Unclosing" first appeared in *The Maine Review*.

About Atmosphere Press

Atmosphere Press is an independent, full-service publisher for excellent books in all genres and for all audiences. Learn more about what we do at atmospherepress.com.

We encourage you to check out some of Atmosphere's latest releases, which are available at Amazon.com and via order from your local bookstore:

Report from the Sea of Moisture, poetry by Stuart Jay Silverman

White Snake Diary, nonfiction by Jane P. Perry

From Rags to Rags, essays by Ellie Guzman

The Enemy of Everything, poetry by Michael Jones

Giving Up the Ghost, essays by Tina Cabrera

The Stargazers, poetry by James McKee

The Pretend Life, poetry by Michelle Brooks

Minnesota and Other Poems, poetry by Daniel N. Nelson

Interviews from the Last Days, sci-fi poetry by Christina Loraine

Unorthodoxy, a novel by Joshua A.H. Harris

the oneness of Reality, poetry by Brock Mehler

Drop Dead Red, poetry by Elizabeth Carmer

Aging Without Grace, poetry by Sandra Fox Murphy

No Home Like a Raft, poetry by Martin Jon Porter

Adrift, poetry by Kristy Peloquin

About the Author

Jessica Palmer lives with her children in the mountains of North Carolina.

Her work has previously appeared in numerous publications.

CPSIA information can be obtained
at www.ICGtesting.com
Printed in the USA
LVHW090330250720
661451LV00005BA/750